UNTERGANG

DAVID BATTEN

Published by Cinnamon Press
Meirion House
Tanygrisiau
Blaenau Ffestiniog
Gwynedd, LL41 3SU
www.cinnamonpress.com

The right of David Batten to be identified as author of this work has been asserted by him in accordance with the Copyright, Designs and Patent Act, 1988. Copyright © 2018 David Batten.
ISBN: 978-1-78864-013-8

British Library Cataloguing in Publication Data. A CIP record for this book can be obtained from the British Library.
All rights reserved. No part of this publication may be reproduced, stored in a retrieval system, or transmitted in any form or by any means, electronic, mechanical, photocopying, recording or otherwise without the prior written permission of the publishers. This book may not be lent, hired out, resold or otherwise disposed of by way of trade in any form of binding or cover other than that in which it is published, without the prior consent of the publishers.

Designed and typeset in Palatino by Cinnamon Press. Printed in Poland.

Cover design by Adam Craig.

Cinnamon Press is represented in the UK by Inpress Ltd and in Wales by the Welsh Books Council.

Acknowledgements

Thanks are due to the editors of the following journals in which some of these poems have appeared: *Dawntreader, Envoi, The French Literary Review, Sarasvati, The Seventh Quarry*.

Thanks as ever to Jan and all at Cinnamon Press.

Notes to Poems

Valkyrie 'Operation Valkyrie' was the name given to the July plot of 1944 to assassinate Hitler.
'not a whole man'—Stauffenberg had lost an eye, his right hand and two fingers from the left hand in 1942, fighting in Tunisia.
The Yeats poem alluded to is 'The Second Coming'.

Hen 'Hen' is Welsh for old. I notice in Glaswegian vernacular it is used a term of endearment for a female (viz. Rab C. Nesbitt).

Untergang The Auden poem alluded to is 'The Shield of Achilles'.

Contents

Visitation	9
Sunday Apéro	10
Fragile Gods	11
Tremor	12
Schopenhauer says	13
You left	14
Portal	15
Lamb	16
Giboulée de mars	17
Firecrest	18
Poems	19
Otherworld	20
New Ways of Describing Blue	21
Solar Power	22
Listening to Prokofiev	23
Prospectus	24
Woodman	25
V.E. Day	26
Fever	27
The Big Six O	28
Elections	29
Invasions	30
Was it you	31
Repas Des Chasseurs	32
Ram	33
Spore	34
Harvest Festival	35
A summer storm	36
World Cup	37
Moon Morning	38
Juliette	39
Valkyrie	40
It approaches—	41
Good Weekend	42

August 1914	43
Hen	44
Close Season	45
Seeing It Through	46
In the dark cauldron of the valley	47
Scotland 18.09.14, 3 a.m.	48
Cascade Du Déroc — A Lover's Leap	49
Laying Out the Year	50
Arddwyn	51
In the Valley of the Lot	52
Contact	53
The Fall	54
Ribs in Space	55
At Neuville St. Vaast	56
On the Somme	57
Rise of the Rat	58
Mythic	59
Trig Point	60
Moorland Fugue	61
The Great Escape	62
Untergang	63
Wintering	64

For Anne Cluysenaar

# Untergang

Visitation

after Ted Hughes

Dreaming Earth turns, dragging down night—
cover for arrival of visitors.
Flames stand suddenly tall in their terror—
trembling alert they feel it first.
Something imminent stirs.
Wind whips up the fire, sucking
the spirit from the room—torpor
from food and booze,

our solstice stupor. Tiny tornadoes
circumnavigate the house
scattering gravel fusillading nerves.
A volt of blue lightning
shoots through its whip-crack of doom,
rattling the lamps.
But as soon as they arrive, they're gone.

Stilled, listening, we feel passed over,
spared, blessed. Around midnight
I step outside in search of the moon.
It's calm. Holy. Our new-year world
glowing white and as surprising to me
as getting this far—mid-term turbulence
quieted by a cosmic blanket furled
over the wake of powers passing through.

Sunday Apéro

Low-angled midday rays
flow through the café.
The glare of January
bombards faces, creased-up
like witnesses to the birth
of some awful weapon.

As le patron winds down a shutter,
shadow creeps along the bar—
from Big Bang to this
private eclipse

light's memory refracted
and spangled in bottles,
crystal's compressed secrets
lined up on shelves.

No one trusts it.

In the hushed saloon,
darkened figures raise
fistfuls of diamonds,
a toast before the meal—

to life, light,
the mysteries of a new year.

Fragile Gods

Two millimetres more tread
off the winter tyres, I'm told,
will imperil our drive home over snow,

while somewhere a universe collapses
haemorrhaging light and heat
into the bullet's black tunnel,

a weakness in the heart, stomach wall,
blood vessel in the brain,
wandering virus randomly locked-on,

circuitry failing,
the whole thing crashing
                       frame
                              by frame,
a mere mild winter
caving in, favouring other life forms.

God's no interest in salvation or old toys.
Before the gaze of unseeing eyes
he's pulling down our stone crosses and spires
in holy all-knowing ignorance.

The sun sets.

The moon sets.

Only stars stare out the black tides.

Tremor

Could be a fortress this house of stone,
yet walls a metre thick trembled
communing with temper passing under

where a man's drowning eyes blood-rimmed
peered from a face of yellowing skin
through the charged air between us over dinner

a tumour doing its corrupt work
where no medicine could work it out—
brilliant organism coral-deadly—

one winter night when our
impregnable house registered
the threat from its submerged tissue.

Schopenhauer says

keep hold of your memories, always,
make them portable
and you can never be completely killed

they're easy to lose —
if you die with none
you die utterly.

My interpretation. Meanwhile
we're wired-in to the present
caught in the blue light of our handheld dreams.

It's a warning.
The future's slipping away —
forever maybe, slipping away.

You left

before the snow fell
before I realised
I should have stopped you

now everything's wrong—
white darkening
becomes epic

visibility
and temperature fall
so fast I imagine

an Antarctica
frostbite
howling wolves

mammoth bones.

A snowplough surges past—
lonely giant
roaring into night

Portal

Awake in the panic hours
to gales of Atlantic anger
ranging inland pummelling our walls.

It's been a grey week of
seamless cloud-pour
portending no good.

Lying in the dark,
a punch bag of worries until
here on the window's black canvass

Van Gogh's huge stars swirl
above atmospheric turmoil.
And there to the east,

Dali's carefree moon-hammock
low-slung above the horizon
beginning its dream-arc into day.

Lamb

still quaking from
the big bang of birth
concentrates its props

rests its head
in my cupped hands
expects to be fed

won't be stroked
quickly works
me out

turns stares about
bewildered
by the valley's bud-

beginnings all new
stunned under sun
valley and lamb poised

this is day one

Giboulée de mars

April shower
a month early
violent downpour
sudden with snow
hail and thunder—
not a crack or peal
seismic
a readjustment
in Lower Ether
pounding valleys
airwaves
tom-tomming bad luck
under grey-black skies
and—just in from
cyberspace as if
from the storm's black heart—
a rejection—
much here we admired.

Pressure lifts.
In the last lick
of winter's hopelessness
I sense summer.

Firecrest

Tiny, with sinister black
burglar band across the eyes
that flame mohican, needle
beak, delicate coral claws.

Punk bird. Amazing make-up
and horror-movie menace
reflected in a membrane
the full-pelt split-second
before dead on a stair.

Weightless in my hand
its substance has left—
no time to linger
birds are busy—this
husk of perfection
a calling card.

Firecrest.

Poems

A graveyard is a book
headstones its pages
true stories a book of lives

as poems
are posthumous
soon as written

are written out lives
of stirrings
that stirred

and stir someone
to commit their souls
to words

words pressed
in a book of deaths
likenesses not as true

as the plastic flowers
nodding in agreement
with their own fake perfection

markers nonetheless that we live
love are moved
from a date to a date

requiems for the living
for the space between
once upon a time and the end

Otherworld

At the very edge of my attention—
in front, where I was not looking—
a stag took me in
and I entered the stillness.

Then a kind of bark, rasp unanimal
repeated, dismantled mantra
too awful to frighten, conducted
through his steadfast form—

cortex to cortex
the hairs on my arms my neck.
I sat down—
the word *scared* passing into *sacred*—

while all around
crackled the immense work of forests

New Ways of Describing Blue

Are there any?

It's cold. The sun breaks through
at twenty degrees
but it's cold. And blue.

At my feet
the dazzle of dandelion outdoes the green
in pleading its case.

But, fixed under an impressive dome,
blue clamping horizons,
the colour of it fraying

the edge of pure clear black
the realm of zero, vacuum
light-years flying in the medium of suns.

That kind of blue.

Solar Power

On a wooded valley slope
stone-aged stones—star grains—
falling

ancient handiwork moss-jacketed
tree-speared-through
unpicking itself.

Long melted,
the erectors
under the hand-placed stones

prised free of winter's grip
called down by the stream
washing, caressing their kin,

splitting-off minerals, nudging,
reworking a whole scarp of stone
to the world's great project.

It will succeed.
The sea wants it.
Gravity wants it.

The seasons assist.
The sun will be satisfied.

Listening to Prokofiev

Russia—winter ice sleigh bells
birch woods black white. But it's the red
in *la Russie—russe rouge roux rousse—*
la lune rousse russet rust—the red
of my mother's hair in my blond beard,
a celtic trace, sandstone smudge
on the wall of a cave, western sunsets
drawing us from eastern waste
to brink of Europe—piling into
peninsulas the ancestral hordes.

What was our dread? What awful
visions had we there
to follow a sinking lure
to the edge of our world?
The spread of Siberia?
Our eastern star in forsaken space
a suspended tear, our freight
a melancholy packed deep and safe—

even from ourselves.

Prospectus

What is it April knows that it postpones
our celebrations? Cold, wet days,
snow on the hills. All-round discouragement.

Yesterday, a technicolour month with
a bluebird on a shoulder. Yesterday,
my father's voice singing *Easter Parade*,
excitement mounting to Cup Final Day.

Today, grim-set faces await figures
to see what cashflow projections will say
about short-term horizons
the nations' cut-and-paste diagnoses.

April takes stock, prepares the ground,
invokes summer under a dangerous moon.
Plant, plant if you dare.

Woodman

His hands are leathered
who cuts the sun-cast trees
autumn and spring before
and after the welling of sap.
And all protection of location
is against the north.
But when the east wind drives in
flame lingers coldly in the stove.

Then he works to keep warm.
Loaded with charms—
wind-burned face smooth
and tough as birch bark
those animal skin hands
wood knowledge—
his wild wood roots—
he enters the fabric of the forest.

Aborigine without heirs
even as we watch he is fading
carbonising
with Cro-Magnon and Celt—
into us—
flame-licked shadows sooted
on a skull wall cosmorama

V.E. Day

and the industrial millions pause.
Sons of Rome, sons of Luther
inheritors of Calvin, Wesley,

do solemnly swear on a book
to love their enemies—it's very clear—
then continue the fight heavenwards

against scapegoats and threats
while the West weeps
over the two thousand years of it,

the stinging salt-laden oceans
filling up, swaying in lamentation
deafening even the deaf.

Fever

A large deer in her summer reds plunged
from right to left like a great fish
through surf of seedheads and grasses

crashing in the oceanic breeze
countryside drunk on pollen
and humidity, the May release

of locked-in life towards its star.
And now the oak beam above my head
moves in woozy perpetual motion

from right to left, by way of
single malt, stress-busting
mind medication and painkiller

after a fall in the shower—
left foot slipped as I dried
the right—how awkwardly I ended,

which makes me contemplate
my own exit and the graceful
arcing flow of a deer in flight.

The Big Six O

and the great project to fend off
anxiety—preoccupation with
pensions and other arrangements.

Before the young, a marketing masterclass
touting a world in the palm—
buy us because you can
your debt is our command.

Then a conjuring trick—miracle
of the age—the cloth pulled out
from under standing lives,

wobbling the china. No time
for remembrance or recrimination—
even the cenotaphs serve the zeitgeist.

The planet revolves, ageing away
from its sun to a moon-desert destiny
as our time washes over the surface
with its mucal blink.

Elections

In his mind's dreaming eye,
George Orwell saw crushed skulls
beneath that fascist step.
Unmistakable. Europa remembers
what her people dare forget.

From Artois to Volga the ground revives,
markets boom and bust drowning warning cries.
And memory, the muffled millions.
Again the concocted pigment of flags
of legitimacy, lineage.

Where are we in all this?
Who plundered our cache of kindness
how did we arrive on this ledge,
our migrations criminalised, our roles
reduced to digital relevance?

As the new century's dawn recedes,
hear ancestors howl and weep,
an oratorio of love—
grunts and gutterals,
clicks and pleadings

through molten whisperings
of Kiev Hamburg Caen—
the return of droning formations
raining the creative fire
of old beginnings.

Invasions

June kicks off
the last anchorings of winter,
chocks away
moorings unmoored.

In a forest clearing pungency
of wild garlic, gougings
of animals, the soft peaty floor
under ripping aerial attack.
Sun, wind and rain knead,
badger and boar tear up
and devour roots glutting
on the vulnerable land.

In other Junes
silent armies, bogged
down with munitions,
clog the midnight piers
under murmurings of last rites
for a morrow of thunder and fire.

So begins and ends
a thousand year feud
between Norman and Saxon
before the gape and sorrow
of a sucked-in world,

its generations
digging for generations
out of the rubble
of their achievements.

Was it you

I found in a storm
fluffed-up proud
grounded cheeping
at the strangeness

and put safely
in a nest, parents
dancing distractedly
about a giant

in gale-force winds
who some time later
fluttered new-fledged wings
to kiss open heavy lids

in a dozing face and
perched on my knee
for unending seconds
eyed me up?

I want to think so.

Repas des Chasseurs

A three-quarter midday moon,
numbskull fixed
in travelling eggshell blue,
bulging Humpty brow pausing

over the hunters' hog,
a hundred and twenty kilos
of pure wild flavour
roasting since dawn
pastis and gentiane apéritifs,
cheese au lait cru, wine
coffee, sugar lumps
dunked in eau de vie,
the Mayor's drapeau and shield
high on the pine—
emblems and souvenirs—

and all the while
children imbibe
the manners
of what they become.

The moon moves on
as it must,
silvering-up nicely
in the heraldic dusk.

Ram

Greek paragon shorn of curls, de-horned,
fitted round the neck with a bell
that crashes into my reading,
my dreaming—portable clanging hell.

What did he do to be so damned?
Ball sock swinging in part orbit
under grass-fed meat seems
innocent enough yet tolls his downfall—

too much jealous independent force—
so the farmer's done for the dignity
of a June-packed munition, tick-
twitching, strapped to its own warning,

all moves registered and rung in pulses
through blood-beating brain
to the black clot sunburst
in its dome

reined in,
head bowed
to the manic praying of crickets.

Spore

I haven't been to this familiar place
before. I float as through a dream
into not another but a new June—
speck on the ring of a planet
of another huge planet
turning towards a new death,
certainly. Rebirth—possibly.

I'm enveloped in a mystery woven
from filaments of a universe,
mantle I wear in reverence
for all I will never understand
as I drift across magnetic fields
of its homeland.

Harvest Festival

for Camille

A poem came my way today—
I carelessly let it go.
It left me behind listening
to pumped waves of accordion
that once brought maidens
in summer frocks to shy
sun-burnished cultivars
following their fathers' ways,
raising cattle, cutting hay—
human achievement,
life grafted onto a plateau
of cooled baked basalt.

We sit down to eat
the traditional feast,
talk of water sources
mushrooms and deer
the class of '62
that left for Paris that year.

Later, on the dance floor
ladies go through time-honed steps
in the echoing hall
whirling ghosts of girls
turning in the night
like lost poems.

A summer storm

blows away a week. Weather fronts
wrestle and bump off each other,
prowl around.

Broiling cloud runs through its rosary—
seven levels of darkness
seven of light—writhing,

wringing itself out over
something in the balance.
Occult forebodings in script

older than worlds,
bright-scribbled across the cortex
fly to earth. Pandemonium

of stars pounding matter, poleaxes
the brain on its quaking root.
Only memory in its reservation—

the deaf mass of mountains
the blind shadow of forests—is unmoved
under sun-moon disturbance.

World Cup

Through the miracle
of electricity
fantasia

a passion played out
by heroes and cheats
the winners

as mystified
as the losers
defeated

when the curtain falls
and one team bows
with nowhere left to go

Moon Morning

Lonely goddess
always somewhere—
if we have treasure it is you.

But you will not be fixed.
Already dismissed,
I imagine your new arrival—

the ocean of sky—
infinity's deep
seems empty with you gone.

Juliette

Six months into her posthumous life,
a man's raw eyes peer
from the chilled gloom of a future.

And for a frozen moment
in a time-blackened room,
shuttered against summer,

they tell an agony of emptiness,
of nothing to do,
how the depeopled village

has betrayed him,
strained his heart, condemned
to this cell of dead friends

and Juliette.
Our presents merge
over a shared bottle of beer.

We drink a toast to all that's left
and all that was here—
Juliette. Juliette!

Valkyrie

after W.B. Yeats

July. Stifling, humid, heavy,
Germany sweating, the world
closing in. Windows open for air,
for overhearing plotting and planning
in The Map Room of The Wolf's Lair.

Their hour come round at last,
Christ and Satan wait in the wings,
totally committed under their
indifferent God, yet still unsure
which way they want this to go.

Stauffenberg is sure, by now ascendant—
not a whole man, not wholly rooted here
in the madness and fear, so not afraid
when the shed explodes, takes to the sky,
breathes the oxygen of a job well done,

the smell of freedom, the lunatic gone
and looks down on his beloved land from
the slow-humming Heinkel churning towards
Berlin. Christ and Satan turn to leave,
noting each other's uncertainty.

It approaches—

I approach it. This
is confusing.

Friends, relatives succumb.
Succumb—fine word for
the process. Receipt.

Death sends symbols, clues—
severed ear, a scorched crow
posted down the flue.

Nearly bumped into
each other recently
at the top of the stair—

both looked away
pretending innocence
pretending ignorance.

Obstinacy of life
randomness of death—
have I understood this

the right way round? No such
conundrum for the doe
who pinpoints me with her

large ears, eyes, nose,
lets me get close,
then steps through the hedgerow

where no gap seems to exist—
two souls on the finite path
between infinities.

Good Weekend

i.m. Guy Vioulac

Though one of us
is missing, we eat,
drink, laugh our way
to honour the absent

and, being older, sadder,
the beer washes
nothing away,
draws absence closer,

until there, among us,
the intoxication of friendship
completes the team
for a fine moment.

A good weekend. But
we're not whole, not really,
beached here by chance
viewing the shining reaches'

incoming tide—
rest of our lives—
blithe interlude erased
for Monday morning's blank page.

August 1914

after Solzhenitsyn

How Russia rejoiced
when war was declared,
her hurrahs echoed in
Paris, London, Berlin,
the rulers' failures cheered
to their heavens

in the name of
the nations' gods—
the God-appointed
on earth—Kaiser,
King, President, Czar—
the apparent flaw

unapparent. Then
she unravels—
still unravelling—
happy atoms
of optimism
marched into August

in some magnetic
order disordered
demagnetised—icons
quake, an empire
implodes, internally
floating apart.

A month examined.
Before the muddied
manoeuvrings of Marne,
Vimy, Somme, a Russian
quantum event.
Clear as vodka.

Hen

for Simone

An old lady calls her chickens
in from the advancing storm

glouc-glouc glouc-glouc
                        glou-ooo

mixes with thunder barrelling
along the valley over
the forsaken farmstead where she grew

glouc-glouc glouc-glouc
                        glou-ooo

more familiar to these trees
these stones
than the waiting car's ticking engine

implying she must hurry
implying time is running out
for a part of us we lose

glouc-glouc glouc-glouc
                        glou-ooo
glouc-glouc glouc-glouc
                        glou-ooo

Close Season

The fixed numbers cinematically
fly off the calendar.
Unable to keep track,
lassitude sets in.

September backs up
like a monstrous seventh wave,
shortening the horizon.
Something will happen—

always happens—returning
energy flows, new projects
from crises gestating
in a pre-season despond.

So sit back,
mix another martini,
il n'y a pas de feu —
count the waves in.

Seeing It Through

A storm's civil war pushed up close
with a mighty show. Night lightnings
daubed the southern sky with warnings—

doomsday masterpieces from east to west,
ground zero to stratosphere. The sizzling
airwaves broadcasting anger.

Then silent nothing, an empty horror,
even the wind flees, stunned stillness
of terrain entering a new era.

The days' shortenings accelerate—
ice and snow will come. Already hard
to recall salamandrine summer.

The seasons' gods take a break while we
negotiate a greying area's greying edge—
strange frontier, we see right through.

In the dark cauldron of the valley

something simmering—
autumn brews.

Pitiless science mixes its potions
invoking the heatless reaches of space
under a chill screen of spun ghost—
connivance with sun against leaf
collaboration with moon
in favour of cool meditation.

Afternoons, all is forgotten.
Blazed-off mists
reveal hillsides still in summer—
naive Eden yielding elderberry,
blackberry, apple, pear,
chestnut, walnut, mushroom.

But behind it all,
power prepares its regime.
Above the river awaiting ice,
ectoplasm negotiates with the stars
by degrees—
how long, how cold, how white—

how clear-eyed the night sky—
how accommodating.

Scotland 18.09.14, 3 a.m.

So what do you say, Scotland,
now your history has stepped
out of its shadow?

Big Money says no. Elites say no—
better together (though
not with Europe).

And what do the glens say,
what do the bloodlines say
murmuring on the salt-tanged air,

the mist out on the loch,
the ringing pines,
the shrieking peat and clashing rocks?

Their skirling song no bagpipe cliché.
It's Scotland.
Scotland!

Cascade du Déroc—A Lover's Leap

Under pressure since ice crashed into
the warm young body,
a torrent springs from Earth's side,

suddenly over a void—a moment's
suspension on air, no way back,
exhilarated with light,

then momentum is ripped from below,
water threatened by light and air
with obliteration, splits,

smashes on rock, regroups,
diminished but undiverted
from its journey back to the sky.

An old stump of brain tells your stomach
to turn before miasma coaxes you
into the same experience,

a fast elevator arriving at your floor,
fluids still rising,
now in reverse—

original magnetism
drawing you down
to the dangerous magic of this place.

Laying Out the Year

Suddenly angled sharp
September light strips back August glare—

sapphire-edged, pares light back
to essentials, Earth's primary colours.

Winter's avatar-surgeon
probing light with light.

The banzai charges of the months
founder. Casualties and booty pile up.

Stooks await collection,
their shadows bleed down a valley side

towards the bright blade of stream
carefully slicing through Earth bone,

countryside gothic-edged
permanent-inked—defined—

laid out in unbearable detail
the thwarted empire of the year

in preparation for annihilation
in preparation for an inferno of ice

Arddwyn

Too long willing a sale
I now scan for booty I can rob
from my own home
the new occupants won't miss.

But this does not interest you
much less the inglenook I revealed,
like magic, from behind a cloud of soot
that now seems to reproach me so.

Your tilted paintings are quizzical—
what is it you don't understand,
your disappointment, your
inglenook gape? Will my spectre-print
outlast my presence here?

When the dead man
carried down your steep stairs
farted, he was dropped
by the terrified bearers.

He regards me now
as does the woman with twelve children
she crammed in your safe inside.
I kind of admire them.

In the Valley of the Lot

Temple open to the sky—
what do your walls say?

Millions of years in stratified script
limestone's compressed code
Earth's poetry grooved on cliff curves
smoothed by an ancient sea
that scribbled this river signature—

also fashioned me
who walks the gallery
that tells a story
beyond the comprehension
of my bulge-browed family.

It will take millennia to remember
how to understand
what the valley is saying—

encoded stations of the earth
sculpted on walls of a stone passage
from nowhere to nowhere,
for a discerning elite—
sympathetic creatures we used to be.

Contact

Pulled up on the brink of catastrophe—
a gorge, say, or crevasse
that doesn't stop at Earth's core—
gorgeous demons call you down.
Your heart leaps. But something
holds the rest of you on this ledge
unlaunched still
grappling every part of you
something beckoning
crackling
through family fibres
like shocks
moving through time
to nerve endings
this moment of danger
making contact
chieftain and druid
soulmates
dream whisperings
through your bones
genetic codes
your mind's eye
all your moments—
a whispering

be careful
we are also here.

The Fall

Suddenly need to reach out an arm into space
trusting for support
I know is not there.
In this twisting second
I know I am dead if I hit the floor.
Know also—this is not the time.
Then help arrives. The hard edge
of the void smashes a rib but slows me,
flips me round still heading down
until the leading hand
thumping wooden treads
brakes me, just short of the cellar's waiting slab.

You saw my still soles sticking up from the stairwell,
assumed I had died—
then I am before you, upright,
manipulating dislocated fingers
into joint—*pull* I am saying *pull*
as we grapple on the terrace
in autumn morning sun.
You're back from market
in your faux-leather jacket—
tailored for a man,
zipped up to the chin—
that suits you so,
blinking back tears
as you pull and pull for all I was worth.

Ribs in Space

A week after the event
my breathless cries
drive you to take me to a doctor

every unseen
undulation of the road
adding to my agony.

Double-fracture
shows the *echographie* clearly,
a floating *morceau* in between—

two spaced-out lengths of bone
trying to reunite across the dark vacuum
around my heart.

All I can do is outlast the pain.
All I can do is trust for a healing
as I do for so many things these days.

At Neuville St. Vaast

The Doctrine —
its logistics
its slogans
trundling over
the killing fields
from Ypres to Arras.

The British Sector
soaked in sour gas
and calcium
still giving up bones
and belt buckles
inscribed *Gott mit uns*.

Let's hope so.
Meadows staked out
with neat rows
of granite crosses
and white stones
for the despatched

known unto God
unwitting generators
of graveyards and newtowns
cheek by blasted jowl —
now there's a slogan —
business going on as usual

as, it seems
it must.

On the Somme

I come across wreaths
and red dragons
at the base of a tree
realise how lost I am
find the wood's edge
and inch along it while
gloom of day swings
to gloom of night
and on that hinge
can just make out
Acid Copse to my right—
Queens's Nullah
should be dead ahead
and somewhere near there
my car.

In dwindling light
I'm bogged down by
the surface tension
of a disaster that makes
some claim on me—
pull of sodden coat
sucking mud on boots
a scared heart beating
against its cage bars
blood in a muddle
which way to turn
across Death Valley's
darkening terrain
of clods and disinterred
beet-heads?
The thought of my car
and its luxuries
a fogged remembrance
from a fading dream.

Rise of the Rat

A freezing creeps into turf.
Halting, the rat in its burrowing track,
scratching at returning tundra,

can make nothing of sudden iron,
this ice-age memory—gives up
dies back—this was not its deal.

Mild winters change all that. Rats,
lords of the subsoil, undermine the land,
tunnel, gnaw through carrot and cable.

Their multiplications nauseate,
their endurance overwhelms,
the absence of God baffles us.

We cannot compete, our lack
teetering above their kingdom,
their blind screeching energy,

our seething foundations.

Mythic

A vibration—somewhere
between oboe and clarinet—
tunes a frequency to its
existential note *who? who?*
Screeching shrieks
answer in frightful tones.

Owls,
triangulating the valley's darkness,
their thrilling descant resonating
through thick autumnal air,
mutating into unexpected
ululation.

Utterances from the unseen.
These are not birds
not terrestrial—strange lords indeed.

Trig Point

Stronghold clumps of marsh grass,
bogs of liquefied peat,
make this heavy going by foot.

At the Table of Orientation,
arrows fly in all directions,
pointing out we are here
in the tread of Neoliths
skirting ice sheets—
the world's migrating millions.

Moorland Fugue

The strung horizon pulls in,
tight-tuned around a sounding bowl
of peat and heather-lined basalt
for windsong composed
on the moor's stave.

The plateau presses its disc
against starlight,
adds its pock-marked tunes
to the symphony of suns and moons—
drumming, wailing, yammering
from ages of stone, bronze, iron.

Our own world-wide whispering
clickings of command,
air-conditioned cockpit hush—
the two hundred year
crescendo of machine
harmonising the crumbling of leaves—
creaking earth's ringing appeal
in the cosmic anthem.

And from leavened tundra
a culture to produce
the hands of pianists
to play it all back.

The Great Escape

Light seems to be giving up.
Day considers changing sides.
Heat slinks away—sun narrowing
its arc, shortening the line.

Trees withdraw to their inner worlds.
The birds' evacuation manoeuvres
started weeks ago. Life closes down,
digs in, takes cover—even soil plays dead.

Only we remain obliged
to carry on. Otherwise exodus
by a southern corridor, the quiet
flight from night's great pincer movement.

Untergang

after W.H. Auden

Tchaikovsky understood—descending
chords and key changes
heading for the grave.

I scavenge our post-industrial wreckage
for scraps of verse—a wrought piece—
the exhausted heap reflecting

in the shining metal shield, huge now,
where two boys knife a third,
where a bird

has to keep coming back
to be stoned over and over
until we get it.

Tchaikovsky understood.
So did Beethoven.

Wintering

after Sylvia Plath

The skies empty
to a blue-black core.

Flaring sunsets fail
to stem the floodtide of night.

On the brink of January
the worst is feared.

Ground hardens. In a field,
the rat-gnawed smile

of a frozen fawn makes its point.
Our familiars, glutted with hindsight,

are plotting next year
while my broken rib quietly knits

gluing itself together
in the dark—

to the prehistoric drumming
of a patient heart